Occasional Papers
No. 35

International Trade in Banking Services: A Conceptual Framework

Sydney J. Key and Hal S. Scott

Published by
Group of Thirty©
Washington, DC
1991

This paper sets forth a conceptual framework that can be used to analyze the rules that should govern international trade in banking services. A unique feature of this framework, embodied in the "Banking Matrix," is that it relates the choice of rules both to the means by which banking services are provided internationally and to the policy goals countries seek to achieve. The paper also discusses the forum in which countries might adopt rules based on this framework.

Table of Contents

Introduction

The Uruguay Round of trade negotiations within the General Agreement on Tariffs and Trade that has been under way since 1986 includes discussions on liberalization of trade in services in addition to trade in goods. The inclusion of services for the first time in GATT negotiations reflects their increasing importance in international trade, especially over the last decade. Financial services in general, and banking services in particular, are now a significant component of international trade in services, in part because of the growing interdependence of national financial markets.

Principles in Use

The search for principles to govern the provision of financial services by foreign firms, whether located inside or outside the national market of the customers, has taken place in a number of contexts in addition to the GATT negotiations. These contexts have included unilateral national policies toward foreign providers of financial services, bilateral treaties such as the U.S.–Canada Free Trade Agreement, the supranational rules adopted by the European Community (EC), and the multilateral codes of the Organisation for Economic Co-operation and Development (OECD). In the banking sector, the major industrial countries have negotiated informal guidelines covering prudential matters such as minimum capital requirements under the auspices of the Bank for International Settlements (BIS).

In this paper we focus on the principles for regulating the international provision of banking services because of the unique character of such services and because, despite the increasing internationalization of financial services and markets, national regulatory systems still differ substantially. The banking sector of a national economy is a particularly sensitive one. Reserves held by banks have traditionally been used as an instrument of monetary policy, and banks play a key role in the payment system and in financing the real economy by intermediating between savers and borrowers. The latter role depends in part on public confidence in the banking system. The failure of one bank can trigger imitative runs on other banks or a chain reaction of failures through the payment system or through default on interbank obligations. This phenomenon is often referred to as "systemic risk."

For international trade in banking services, the most generally accepted principle is national treatment, which seeks to ensure equality of competitive opportunity for domestic and foreign firms providing banking services in a host country. Under a policy of national treatment, foreign banks are treated as nearly as possible like domestic banks: They have the same opportunities for establishment that domestic banks have, they can exercise the same powers in the host country, and they are subject to the same obligations. But differences between regulatory and institutional structures in home and host countries can make it difficult to apply the principle of national treatment.[1]

Some of the most intractable problems stem from the lack of agreement among the major industrial countries regarding the permissible activities of banks. For example, the European Community finds it difficult to accept U.S. restrictions separating commercial and investment banking in the United States when the Community does not apply such restrictions to the activities of EC banks. Problems also arise in trying to apply to foreign branches capital adequacy and other requirements developed for the domestic banks of a host country. Moreover, national treatment does not address the extent to which multinational cooperation and agreement are necessary to regulate and supervise financial activities conducted internationally.

Other principles for governing international trade in financial services go beyond national treatment, that is, they presuppose national treatment and seek something more. These principles have been advanced as the basis for requirements imposed by national reciprocity policies or as obligations undertaken in connection with international agreements or supranational regulation. Although these principles, with labels such as mutual recognition and effective market access, are not always precisely defined, they involve explicit or implicit harmonization of national regulatory structures, with concomitant changes in the regulation of domestic as well as foreign banks.

The Banking Matrix

In this paper we develop a conceptual framework for analyzing the principles that should govern the provision of international banking services. To do so, we substitute for the conventional terminology more basic, albeit less colorful, terms. National treatment and the principles that go beyond it can be understood in terms of three basic components that can be applied separately or in combination: (1) host-country rules; (2) home-country rules; and (3) harmonized rules that apply in both countries. For example, national treatment requires the nondiscriminatory application of host-country rules to foreign banks. By contrast, mutual recognition, which is the basis of the EC internal market program, involves both harmonization of essential rules and, in the absence of harmonization, acceptance by host countries of home-country rules. Even if rules are harmonized, there is the question of who administers the rules—the host country, the home country, or a supranational entity. In the banking sector, this question is particularly important because harmonization does not by itself guarantee the quality of supervision.

The public policy question is what basic principle or combination of principles—host-country rules, home-country rules, or harmonized rules—should govern international trade in banking services. Our analysis suggests that no single rule is appropriate for the provision of all international banking services. The choice of a rule depends on the interaction between two factors: the manner in which the service is provided and the public policy goals underlying the regulation of banking services. A bank located in one country (the home country) can provide services to customers in another country (the host country) in three principal ways: across borders, that is, without establishing a

3

Banking Matrix

Rules to govern international trade in banking services,
for combinations of policy goals and methods of providing services

| Policy goal | Method of providing banking services | | |
| | | *Branches* | |
	Cross-border	*Entry*	*Operation*
Competitive markets	Home-country rules	Home-country rules and harmonized rules	Home-country rules and harmonized rules
Safety and soundness	Harmonized rules, home-country enforcement of rules	Harmonized rules, home-country enforcement of rules	Harmonized rules, home-country enforcement of rules
Avoidance of systemic risk	Home-country rules	Does not apply	Host-country rules with additional requirements for foreign banks
Consumer protection: Deposit insurance	Home-country rules	Does not apply	Host-country rules with additional requirements for foreign banks, agreement on home-country bankruptcy jurisdiction
Consumer protection: Disclosure	Host-country rules	Does not apply	Host-country rules

<table>
Method of providing banking services	
Subsidiaries	
Entry	*Operation*

Entry	*Operation*
Host-country rules and harmonized rules	Host-country rules and harmonized rules
Host-country rules	Host-country rules
Does not apply	Host-country rules
Does not apply	Host-country rules
Does not apply	Host-country rules
</table>

presence in the host country; through branches established in the host country; or through subsidiaries, which must be separately incorporated in the host country. Countries generally have four principal policy objectives that affect their regulation of such services: promoting competitive markets, ensuring the safety and soundness of banks, protecting against systemic risk, and ensuring adequate protection of consumers.

In regulating the international provision of banking services, countries must choose from among the basic principles the ones most likely to promote these policy goals, given the forms in which banking services are provided. To help organize thinking about these choices, we have constructed a "Banking Matrix," which sets forth the combinations of public policy goals and forms of provision of banking services.

The entries in the cells of the Banking Matrix summarize the results of our analysis. For example, the analysis suggests that the best way to govern the entry of foreign branches so as to promote safety and soundness would be to apply harmonized rules that the home country would enforce. Similarly, consumers would be protected best if subsidiaries of foreign banks operated under host-country rules. The matrix emphasizes a major theme of our analysis, namely, that different principles may be appropriate for different forms of provision of services or for different policy goals. Thus, the matrix indicates that, with some important exceptions, home-country rules should be applied to cross-border services, host-country rules to subsidiaries, and harmonized rules or special host-country rules to branches. It also indicates that harmonized rules are particularly important for the goals of promoting competitive markets and ensuring safety and soundness. Although reasonable people may differ over the particular principles we propose for each cell of the matrix, it is still valuable in relating policy goals to methods of providing services.

The Appropriate Forum

Our analysis suggests that a fully satisfactory international framework for trade in banking services would require countries to agree whether host, home, or harmonized rules should apply in particular situations, and on the specifics of harmonized rules when harmonization is the accepted principle. Since that effort would clearly go considerably beyond the one currently under way in the GATT's Uruguay Round, the paper also discusses the characteristics of a forum in which such agreements might be negotiated.

In principle, the forum would comprise primarily the most developed countries; it would have the participation of finance ministry officials and financial service regulators; and it would possess the authority to formulate proposals, monitor their implementation, and resolve disputes. No such forum exists at present. However, we suggest that the OECD or the GATT might, with some modifications to their current structure, serve as a broad forum for agreement on appropriate principles and could participate in or coordinate the efforts of other specialized fora, such as the BIS Committee on Banking Regulations and Supervisory Practices, in arriving at harmonized rules.

We begin our analysis by discussing the different, and sometimes conflicting, public policy goals that form the vertical dimension of the matrix. Next, for each of the different forms of international trade in banking services, the horizontal dimension of the matrix, we discuss which of the three basic principles, or combination thereof, best furthers each of the policy goals. We then summarize the results by providing generalizations about the appropriate rule for a particular form of provision of services or for a particular policy goal and identifying the areas in which such generalizations break down. Our analysis makes it clear that the provision of international banking services through branches presents the most difficult public policy choices. Finally, we discuss the forum issue, and draw some general conclusions.

Complementary and Conflicting Policy Goals

In this section we review the goals countries generally pursue with respect to banking services and examine how these goals may complement or conflict with one another.

Promoting Competitive Markets

It is generally agreed that free trade results in competitive and efficient markets that maximize consumer welfare. To achieve free trade in banking services, then, what barriers must be removed? Clearly, national rules that *discriminate* between foreign and domestic providers of banking services constitute barriers to free trade. The principle of national treatment, which applies host-country rules to foreign and domestic firms on a nondiscriminatory basis, is meant to ensure equality of competitive opportunity by eliminating such discriminatory barriers. It is generally understood that national treatment must be applied de facto as well as de jure. For example, the OECD National Treatment Instrument defines national treatment as treatment under host-country "laws, regulations and administrative practices…no less favourable than that accorded in like situations to domestic enterprises." The expression "no less favourable" acknowledges that exact national treatment cannot always be achieved and that any adjustment should favor the foreign firm.

But the appropriate market for achieving equality of competitive opportunity for multinational banking institutions may be broader than a single country. Because such banks compete on a global scale, barriers to international trade in banking services may also result from *nondiscriminatory* differences in national rules, that is, differences in national rules that do not discriminate between domestic and foreign firms. Fundamental differences in rules for permissible activities of banks or for the products they may offer can create significant barriers to trade. Even if they are nondiscriminatory, a country's rules may be so much more restrictive than those in other major countries that they create market distortions and inefficiencies. For example, in the view of the

European Community, prohibitions on combining banking and securities activities in the United States and limitations on interest rates in Japan restrict the ability of EC banks to compete effectively in those markets.

Although market forces may foster regulatory convergence in the longer run, in the short term removing nondiscriminatory barriers among countries may be extremely difficult politically. However, within the European Community, where political agreement on goals for regulatory convergence has already been reached, the elimination of nondiscriminatory barriers to trade in banking services is a critical element of the internal market program.[2] This liberalization is being carried out in an environment of substantial coordination and of common obligations established through a supranational structure to which the member states have already transferred a significant degree of sovereignty. By contrast, the OECD Codes of Liberalization and National Treatment Instrument are concerned only with discriminatory barriers, a limitation that reflects the absence of a comparable political consensus or degree of integration among members of that organization. For this reason, a GATT agreement on trade in services would have even more difficulty in addressing nondiscriminatory barriers.

"Reverse discrimination" could occur if foreign banks were to receive treatment better than that granted to host-country banks—if, say, a German bank were permitted to offer a service in France (even when French banks could not do so) on the grounds that Germany permitted the service to be offered. Under the EC internal market program, powers permitted in the home country (provided such activities are listed in the Second Banking Directive) will govern the provision of banking services across borders and through branches. However, the expectation—indeed, the overall EC strategy—is that any resulting competitive inequalities for a host country's banks will quickly force that country to conform its national rules to those of other member states. Within the Community, such reverse discrimination is essentially a strategy to produce harmonization and is predicated on political agreement on goals for convergence of national regulatory systems.

Another dimension of national policies to promote competitive markets involves adoption and enforcement of policies to prevent concentrations of market power ("antitrust policy" in the United States, "competition policy" in the European Community). These policies generally support de novo entry by new competitors, and thus do not pose obstacles to foreign banks offering cross-border services or establishing branches or subsidiaries in host countries. They might prevent a foreign bank that already has a substantial presence in a host country from acquiring a bank of significant size in that country, but such restrictions would apply equally to domestic banks.

Other considerations may sometimes modify—or even overrule—the economic goal of promoting competitive and efficient markets. In particular, developing countries often restrict competition from foreign banks out of concern that those banks will dominate their less efficient domestic institutions. To such countries, the efficiency gains achievable through competition are outweighed by the loss in national control of the banking sector. In some cases, such countries gradually open up their markets as they become more confident about the ability of their local institutions to compete. Industrialized countries are not immune to similar considerations: France and Italy in effect protect some of their major banks from foreign ownership through state ownership of these institutions. The governor of the Bank of England has stated that in the United Kingdom, which is generally regarded as having an open and competitive banking market, "it is of the highest importance that there should be a strong and continuing British presence in the banking system. . . ."[3]

Devising a policy to promote competition in the banking sector through the entry of foreign banks is complicated by the need to ensure the safety and soundness of banks and to protect consumers of banking services. Countries have often justified limits on competition, such as chartering restrictions, ceilings on deposit interest rates, and restrictions on permissible activities, on prudential grounds. Some have argued that less competition means fewer failures. In the international context, countries may fear unfair competition from banks of other countries that regulate their institutions less stringently. Lower home-country capital requirements, for example, may allow foreign banks to operate on narrower margins. Given the significance of financial services to consumers, national legislation to protect consumers is also an important factor. The line between legitimate host-country consumer protection and anticompetitive policies is often hard to draw, particularly when the service provider is foreign and thus may be beyond the reach of the local authorities.

Ensuring Safety and Soundness

Because of concerns about systemic risk and consumer protection countries seek to avoid bank failures through safety and soundness policies. If, for example, capital adequacy requirements provided a 100 percent guarantee that a bank would never fail, other measures to deal with systemic risk or depositor losses would be unnecessary. If a country has a deposit protection scheme, capital and other requirements to ensure the safety and soundness of banks protect the insurer, and possibly the taxpayer, not just the consumer of banking services. In this paper, we view deposit insurance schemes as related primarily to the goal of consumer protection. However, such schemes are usually justified also as ensuring the stability of the banking system. By providing safety for the funds of individual depositors, these schemes protect those who are relatively unsophisticated financially and also reduce the systemic risk resulting from withdrawal of depositors' funds not only from troubled institutions but also from other banks. Some might argue that to the extent a bank is experiencing difficulties solely because it lacks liquidity, a deposit insurance scheme contributes to its safety and soundness. But the U.S. experience suggests that the moral hazard of an overly generous deposit insurance scheme can encourage excessive risk-taking by bank owners and managers and thereby, perversely, undermine the safety and soundness of individual banks.

National authorities impose a variety of rules to ensure the safety and soundness of banks. These include capital requirements, limitations on large exposures, liquidity requirements, restrictions on permissible activities, requirements for accounting that accurately reflect the bank's condition and help to prevent fraud, and requirements for reporting and

11

examination for regulatory and supervisory purposes. Ensuring the safety and soundness of foreign banks providing services in its territory poses special problems for a host country because it does not directly regulate or supervise the foreign parent bank.

This issue frequently arises with regard to branches of foreign banks, whose capital is essentially that of the foreign institution and whose condition is monitored and supervised by home-country authorities. To address this situation, host countries often impose special quasi-capital or liquidity requirements on branches of foreign banks. However, these rules can unduly restrict competition. Unlike most countries, the United Kingdom does not impose such requirements and instead relies on procedures for screening of banks seeking to establish branches in its territory and regular monitoring of branch activities.

One promising approach to ensuring the safety and soundness of foreign banks operating in a host country is to reach international agreement on prudential rules, that is, the harmonization approach. In general, the internationalization of financial services and markets has both necessitated and facilitated international cooperation with regard to supervision and regulation. But the coordination and harmonization of rules have been accomplished by bank regulatory authorities in a relatively limited and informal way. For example, the 1988 Basle risk-based capital framework is an accord among the banking authorities of the major industrial countries rather than a formal international agreement or treaty. It was negotiated under the auspices of the BIS Committee on Banking Regulations and Supervisory Practices, a committee established in December 1974 as a mechanism for regular consultation among the banking authorities of the Group of Ten countries.[4] Two earlier accords had been negotiated in the same way: the 1975 Basle Concordat, which sets forth general principles regarding the relative roles of home- and host-country supervisors in an effort to ensure that all banking organizations operating in international markets are supervised institutions; and the revised Concordat, released in 1983, which incorporates the principle of supervision of multinational banking institutions on a consolidated worldwide basis.[5]

Protecting against Systemic Risk

The need to protect against systemic risk arises because prudential controls may be ineffective in preventing liquidity or solvency problems for a particular institution. In that event, the difficulties of one bank may be transmitted to others, and ultimately affect the banking system as a whole. For example, a failing bank may hold substantial interbank deposits, either as a result of placements or through furnishing correspondent payment services. This was a particular concern in the case of the near failure of Continental Illinois Bank in the mid-1980s. Moreover, if a bank that participates in a net settlement payment system, such as CHIPS in the United States or EAF in Germany, is unable to settle its position, other participating banks may incur losses.[6] A chain reaction could also occur through withdrawal of depositors' funds from the troubled institution and from institutions that have claims on it or that are perceived to be exposed to the same risks.

Domestic regulations may limit the participation of foreign banks in interbank markets or national payment systems in order to minimize the possibility that a foreign bank failure could trigger a series of domestic bank failures. The BIS, through its Committee on Interbank Netting Schemes, has recently set out minimum standards for the design and operation of cross-border and multicurrency netting schemes, as well as principles for cooperative central bank oversight of such schemes.[7] The major purpose of such standards is to minimize the possibility of settlement failures and thereby to limit systemic risk.

Many countries seek to avoid systemic risk by rescuing failing banks. They employ a variety of techniques: extensions of credit by the central bank, injections of capital, arrangement of mergers with healthy institutions. Because such measures are designed to restore the solvency of failing banks, they can be viewed as another aspect of policies to promote safety and soundness. However, because they become necessary only when a bank is in danger of failing, it is useful to distinguish them from the normal prudential regulation and supervision that apply to all banks. In countries with a government-operated deposit insurance scheme, such as the United States, measures for dealing with failing banks may be part of that scheme because the insurer has an interest in the comparative costliness of alternative rescue measures. Nonetheless, rescue measures are widely employed by countries without deposit insurance schemes, and thus we consider such measures as furthering the policy goal of avoiding systemic risk.

Ensuring Adequate Consumer Protection

Consumer protection measures in the banking area generally fall into two broad categories. The first—primarily deposit insurance systems—consists of laws and regulations to limit losses of depositors. Host-country branches of foreign banks may be required to participate in such a system, particularly if they take domestic deposits in the host country.[8] The second category of consumer protection measures consists of disclosure rules. They typically apply to terms of credit, interest rates payable on deposits, charges for checks, and so on. Some countries go beyond simply requiring disclosure and mandate certain provisions in consumer contracts; some countries also try to protect the consumer against unwarranted disclosure of personal financial information.

Consumer protection policies are often politically sensitive. In the European Community, where the basic approach to banking regulation consists of a combination of harmonized and home-country rules with home-country enforcement, consumer protection rules could still be adopted by the host country. However, if such rules create barriers to the provision of banking services by banks from other member states, the host country must be able to justify the restrictions as necessary to protect the "public interest," a stringent standard established by the European Court of Justice. The Court not only requires that host-state restrictions apply equally to foreign and domestic firms, but also prohibits such restrictions if the public interest is already protected by the rules of the home state or if less restrictive rules could achieve the same result.

Maintaining the Effectiveness of Monetary Policy

In the absence of a monetary union, domestic monetary policy is, of course, set and implemented by host countries. Although the provision of international banking services cannot change this basic fact, it does raise the question of whether such policy can be effective. In a world of economically interdependent nations, domestic monetary policy cannot be made in isolation. Over the past few decades, in several fora, the major industrial countries have sought to consult and cooperate with regard to the formulation of macroeconomic policies; during the last five years, among the Group of Seven countries, the process has become somewhat more formal.[9]

Theoretically, international banking activity should not interfere with the conduct of domestic monetary policy in a large open economy. Such activity would not render domestic monetary policy ineffective even though it might change the responsiveness of interest rates to a given change in the monetary base or modify the relationship between a change in interest rates and a change in nominal gross national product. The monetary authorities would still be able to achieve their targets; they would, in effect, adjust their decision making to take into account the effect of the offshore activity. Because the offshore activity could, over time, alter these relationships in unpredictable ways, the availability of data on such activity is helpful. Thus, some countries collect and share information: for example, Canada and the United Kingdom provide the United States with aggregate data on U.S. dollar-denominated deposits of U.S. residents at banking offices in those countries.

In any event, host-country rules, with some degree of international coordination and cooperation, govern the conduct of monetary policy. The use of host-country rules is not dependent on the way in which international banking services are provided, and monetary policy considerations thus should not affect our analysis.

Principles Applicable to Different Forms of Trade in Banking Services

International trade in banking services, as we use the term, refers to provision of banking services by a bank whose principal place of business is in one country to customers in another country. Providing banking services to host-country residents from an office in another country—cross-border provision of services—is analogous to trade in goods. But providing banking services may also involve direct foreign investment if it takes place through a branch or subsidiary in the host country. Thus, rules regarding both the establishment and the operation of host-country offices of foreign banks play an important role in international trade in banking services. Because the different forms of providing banking services pose distinct issues in terms of the public policy goals discussed above, we consider each form separately.

Cross-border Provision of Services

Cross-border services are those offered by a bank located in one country to customers in another country without establishing an office in the customer's country, the host country. In general, the liberalization of cross-border services has concentrated on removing exchange controls. In recent years, however, increased attention has been given to barriers in such areas as portfolio management and investment advice; this shift has been particularly apparent within the OECD, where much of the multinational work on international trade in financial services has taken place. Examples of host-country rules that impede the cross-border provision of services include restrictions on particular products or instruments, prohibitions on the solicitation of business by foreign entities, and tax rules that favor transactions with domestic rather than foreign offices.

The OECD principles for treatment of foreign providers of cross-border services depend on whether the transaction takes place in the host country or abroad. In the first case, the transaction may be significantly regulated but only on a nondiscriminatory basis; in the second, only advertising in the host country may be regulated, but discrimination is not forbidden. Because they are intangible, however, locating the situs of banking services provided across borders is fraught with difficulties. This issue typically arises with respect to tax treatment of cross-border transactions and the choice of law governing a particular transaction. For example, lenders and borrowers can easily adapt to formalistic rules that make tax treatment turn on where a loan agreement is signed.

Competitive markets. In the interest of promoting competitive markets, host countries should allow cross-border provision of services under home-country rules without imposing any restrictions. This practice would permit host-country consumers access to a broader range of services and a larger number of service providers. On the other hand, broader powers, lower capital requirements, subsidies, and other advantages offered by foreign governments may make for "unfair" competition in the context of cross-border services. As discussed below, the Basle risk-based capital accord partially addresses this concern by setting minimum capital requirements for banks in countries party to that agreement. However, if the only consideration were maximizing the welfare of host-country consumers (but not producers), it might be preferable to allow them to benefit from, for example, more favorable pricing by foreign banks, even in the absence of additional harmonization. In any event, for large business customers, host country limitations on the provision of services would be largely ineffective since such customers have easy access to banking offices located abroad. Thus, we conclude that the goal of competitive markets can best be promoted by applying home-country rules, as the Banking Matrix indicates.

Safety and soundness. The host country has a concern with the safety and soundness of foreign banks offering cross-border deposit services to retail customers, who could be defined as those with deposits of, say, under $100,000. Other customers, it is presumed, can protect their own interests and, in any case, can more easily place funds in the Euromarkets. If a foreign bank taking such retail deposits were to fail, host-country customers would be at risk unless the deposit insurance scheme in the home country protected them. However, absent at least some international harmonization of deposit insurance schemes (which we discuss below), a host country could not rely on the adequacy of such a scheme in the home country, even if one existed.

In any event, prudential rules are the first line of defense against bank failures, and the international harmonization of these rules is the most promising approach for ensuring the safety and soundness of a foreign bank providing cross-border services. Harmonization could occur through adherence to the Basle accord by a broader group of countries or by the host-country conditioning acceptance of retail deposits on the home country's adherence to the accord. To further the goal of safety and soundness, we therefore envision international harmonization, as depicted in the Banking Matrix.

Since the service provider is located entirely abroad, only the home-country regulators could enforce the international standards. Ensuring some degree of uniformity in the enforcement of such standards would depend primarily on cooperation and consultation among supervisors. In this regard, it should be noted that the "home-country" supervisors might include not only those from the place of incorporation or location of the entity providing the service but also those from the country in which the banking organization as a whole has its principal place of business. This would also be the case with respect to branches and subsidiaries, discussed below.

Avoiding systemic risk. A host country has minimal concern with systemic risk in the provision of cross-border services. The risk for individual domestic banks of holding deposits with foreign banks can be addressed by regulating such exposure directly rather than by imposing restraints on foreign banks. Cross-border services do not directly involve a foreign bank in the payment system of the host country, nor is the failure of a foreign bank likely to trigger imitative runs on domestic banks. If such runs were to occur, they would, in any case, have little relation to the foreign bank's provision of cross-border services. Thus, home-country rules should apply with respect to systemic risk, as noted in the matrix.

Consumer protection. For cross-border services, deposit insurance must necessarily be provided under the home country's scheme. The host country could, of course, best protect its consumers if basic elements of deposit insurance schemes were harmonized among nations. But achievement of this goal, although highly desirable, seems unlikely given the vast disparities in these schemes. Furthermore, the enormous effort that would be required to achieve harmonization does not seem justified by the host country's policy concern with insurance of its residents' deposits in foreign offices of foreign banks. Therefore, home-country rules, without any harmonization, should govern deposit insurance for cross-border provision of services.

By contrast, host-country rules can be used for disclosure requirements or mandatory contract terms. For example, host countries could require a foreign bank to disclose whether its deposits are insured and, if so, by whom and on what terms. If the deposit were denominated in a foreign currency, disclosure of the currency risk might also be required. Such rules would not impose extra requirements on foreign banks because they would be associated with the nature of the transaction, not with the nationality of the provider. Thus, domestic banks that offered foreign currency deposits would be subject to the same disclosure rules about exchange risk. In contrast to the OECD approach, determining the situs for provision of the service would not be important. If host countries were to impose overly burdensome disclosure requirements or mandatory contract terms, there might be a need to harmonize these measures to avoid an adverse impact on competition. However, for purposes of this paper, we assume such harmonization would not be necessary.

Branches

Traditionally, analyses of issues relating to international trade in banking services have distinguished between providing services across borders, on the one hand, and providing them through the establishment of subsidiaries or branches, on the other. But a further distinction is useful because, unlike a subsidiary, a branch is an integral part of the foreign bank and is not separately incorporated in the host country. Recently, the special characteristics of branches have been given increased attention in international fora such as the OECD. Moreover, the European Community has in effect drawn a line between financial services provided through subsidiaries (which are subject to nondiscriminatory host-country rules) and those provided through branches and cross-border services (which are governed by home-country rules and enforcement, based on harmonization of essential rules). Our analysis seeks to identify the rules that should be applicable to the establishment (entry) of branches and to their operation.

Entry. Only two of the policy goals we have identified seem relevant for the entry of branches of foreign banks: competition, and safety and soundness.

COMPETITIVE MARKETS. Some countries limit or prohibit entry by branches of foreign banks by, for example, applying quotas or limitations on geographic location that do not apply to domestic banks. Developing countries often impose restrictions out of fear of foreign domination, although developed countries may also restrict branch entry. Canada, for example, prohibits the establishment of branches of foreign banks, although it would justify the prohibition on grounds of safety and soundness.

Because branches can operate on the basis of the consolidated capital of the foreign bank and are often a more efficient method of doing business than operating through subsidiaries, permitting branch entry is important in promoting competition among foreign and domestic banks in a host-country market. This consideration suggests that, for competitive purposes, branches should be allowed to enter under home-country rules; that is, if the home country authorizes a bank to establish a foreign branch, the host country would be required to accept that decision. Safety and soundness concerns would be addressed by harmonization of prudential standards (see discussion below).

A further problem arises with respect to nondiscriminatory restrictions imposed by a host country. For example, a host country such as the United States may restrict *intra*national branching of its own banks and, accordingly, also place geographic limitations on the establishment of branches of foreign banks. Even if they are nondiscriminatory, such limitations may be anticompetitive and create barriers to the provision of banking services, both on an intranational and international basis. This type of problem could be resolved through international harmonization of rules for intranational geographic expansion.

In view of these considerations, home-country and harmonized rules appear to be the best way to promote competitive markets with regard to the establishment of branches, as reflected in the Banking Matrix. Thus, home-country rules would be used to determine whether a foreign bank was permitted to establish branches in the host country. Harmonization of prudential standards would remove the safety and soundness justification for discriminatory host-country restrictions. Harmonization is included under the goal of competitive markets to deal with a different issue, namely, the elimination of nondiscriminatory barriers to branch entry.

SAFETY AND SOUNDNESS. Prudential concerns regarding entry of foreign branches cannot be allayed by the nondiscriminatory application of host-country law. Allowing entry by a foreign branch is inherently different from permitting a domestic bank to open a branch. Branching by a domestic bank is predicated on initial approval for the establishment of the bank itself, and establishment of a branch is merely incremental. Moreover, domestic banks are subject to domestic (host-country) regulation for safety and soundness, whereas a foreign bank establishing a branch is not. The host country therefore needs to assure itself on this point in permitting entry for a foreign branch.

When a country permits entry by a foreign branch, it is implicitly or explicitly accepting the adequacy of home-country regulation and supervision, including enforcement of those rules. But why should it accept the adequacy of regulation and supervision by all home countries? Some degree of harmonization of rules—say, by adherence to the Basle accord or other internationally agreed standards—might be required before permitting entry. Even if rules were harmonized, a host country might have reservations about the quality of enforcement in a particular home country; but conditioning entry on the quality of supervision would be extremely difficult unless home-country supervision was extraordinarily lax. The only answer may be sufficient cooperation and consultation among national supervisory authorities to establish an atmosphere of mutual trust.

The approach of harmonization with home-country enforcement is reflected in the Banking Matrix. By removing the safety and soundness justification for discriminatory restrictions on entry, international harmonization of prudential rules would enable nations to permit branches of foreign banks to enter under home-country rules, and would thereby promote competitive markets.

Operation. In contrast to entry, the operation of branches raises issues for all four of the policy goals.

COMPETITIVE MARKETS. Competition within a host-country market would be promoted by allowing branches of foreign banks to engage in the same activities permissible for domestic banks, that is, by a policy of national treatment. However, competition could be further promoted if branches of foreign banks were allowed to engage in any activities their home countries permitted. If home-country rules were the more liberal ones, host-country banks would suffer reverse discrimination that could be removed only by a change in the host-country rules. However, if home-country rules were more restrictive than host-country rules *and* the home country applied identical rules to its banks' foreign and domestic activities, branches of home-country banks would be at a competitive disadvantage in the host-country markets.

The European Community is using the home-country approach, but bases that approach on agreement among countries regarding convergence of national rules. Thus, the EC's Second Banking Directive involves both harmonization and home-country rules.[10] It sets forth a list of activities subject to mutual recognition; a host country is required to permit a bank from another member state to engage, through a branch or through the cross-border provision of services, in any activity on the list that the home country permits. Without implicit or explicit agreement on such a list, it would be politically impossible, either within or beyond the Community, to allow branches of foreign banks to operate under home-country rules for permissible activities.

Home-country rules combined with harmonization of basic rules for permissible activities would best promote competitive markets for operation of branches, and this is reflected in the Banking Matrix. Such harmonization could be explicit, as in the European Community, or it could occur de facto through unilateral changes in national rules to conform to the more liberal rules in other countries. However, a broader group of countries may find it difficult to agree on permissible activities, especially securities activities or insurance activities (the latter are not even included on the EC's list). Countries have different traditions and experience in this area. Some view expansion of bank powers as a positive promotion of competition; others have concerns about safety and soundness, potentially anticompetitive concentrations of power, or conflicts of interest.

At present, two major countries with restrictive rules for permissible activities—Japan and the United States—are considering proposals for change. However, adoption of these proposals would not produce the harmonization necessary to allow branches of foreign banks to operate under home-country rules for permissible activities. The reason is that the proposals envision that securities and insurance activities would be conducted in affiliates of the bank rather than in the bank itself. This approach contrasts with that of the European Community, discussed above, under which securities activities (though not insurance activities) could be conducted in the bank. As a result, a second-best alternative to the entry in the Banking Matrix—that is, home-country and harmonized rules for permissible activities of branches—would be host-country rules for permissible activities of branches combined with harmonized rules for permissible activities of bank affiliates. Such harmonization would, in effect, require implicit or explicit agreement on a list of permissible activities for bank affiliates. There would also need to be agreement that foreign banks could operate such affiliates in addition to branches in a host country.

SAFETY AND SOUNDNESS. The issue of safety and soundness with regard to operations of branches of foreign banks in a host country is similar to that with regard to entry. Once a branch was permitted to enter, its safety and soundness would continue to be determined largely by harmonized standards enforced by the home country. If, in the absence of a more widespread international agreement, adherence to the Basle standards by the parent bank had been a condition of entry, continued adherence should be included as part of the condition. As in the case of entry, the issue of adequate enforcement of harmonized standards could be dealt with through cooperation and consultation among national supervisors. In the extreme case, branch activities could be terminated by host-country authorities.

SYSTEMIC RISK. Considerations of systemic risk are of particular significance for branches of foreign banks because the failure of a foreign bank necessarily means that its branches cannot continue to operate. The inability of a branch that played a significant role in host-country financial markets to meet its obligations could lead to a chain reaction of failures of other banks through the interbank market or payment and settlement systems or through imitative runs on branches of other foreign banks and on domestic banks. If a home country rescues a failing bank, systemic risk can be avoided; but host countries cannot count on such rescues. The decision of a country to rescue a failing bank depends on a variety of considerations, including the immediate financial cost and the longer-term potential for increasing moral hazard.

If necessary, the interbank market problem can be addressed by prudential regulation of domestic banks, for example, by limiting large exposures to less creditworthy banks, whether domestic or foreign. The risk to domestic banks from the failure of a foreign bank would generally not increase because funds were placed with a host-country branch of that bank rather than with the foreign bank in its home country or with a branch in a third country.

The payment and settlement system of a host country is subject to two risks from foreign branches. First, a foreign branch might default on a settlement position through failure to cover uncollateralized over-drafts on its clearing account with a central bank, incurred in connection with the use of a central bank payment system, such as FedWire in the United States. Such a failure might result in a loss for the central bank. Second, the failure of a foreign branch to meet its uncollateralized settlement obligations in a net settlement system, such as CHIPS in the United States, could expose other bank participants to losses.

Given that the ability of foreign branches to meet their settlement obligations depends ultimately on the solvency of the bank as a whole, which is regulated by the home country, host countries may be reluctant to allow foreign branches to participate in their payment systems on the same terms as domestic institutions. In addition, branches of foreign banks may have more difficulty than domestic institutions do in promptly covering settlement shortfalls: They may be less able to fund themselves quickly in host-country money markets, and home-country markets could be closed. The costs of settlement failure could be avoided if a central bank were to extend lender-of-last-resort facilities to the failing bank. But it is not clear whether any central bank would make these facilities available in such a situation. And then, which central bank would do so—that of the home country of the failing bank or that of the country in which the payment system operates?

The risks that participation by branches of foreign banks pose to a payment system could be controlled by a variety of measures. The BIS Report has formulated minimum standards for the G-10 countries that are designed to minimize the possibility of a settlement failure in net settlement systems. These standards would affect all participants in such systems, whether branches of foreign banks or domestic institutions. Although adoption of these standards will decrease the risk of settlement failure, it will not eliminate it. Moreover, the standards do not apply to use of central bank gross payment systems, such as FedWire, so that other policy measures will still be required.

One approach is to exclude branches of foreign banks from direct participation in the payment system by requiring them to clear payments through domestic participants. France, for example, permits only domestic banks to participate in Sagittaire, its net settlement system for cross-border payments. Alternatively, branches of foreign banks could be subject to special position limits or collateral requirements. Although such requirements could be viewed as discriminatory, they may be the only practical alternative to a system under which the host country's central bank may be forced to act as a lender of last resort for such branches. The Banking Matrix therefore indicates that host-country rules should apply with respect to systemic risk, with the qualification that the rules for branches of foreign banks may be different from those for domestic banks.

Harmonization might be used to avoid special requirements for branches. For example, the Federal Reserve Board in the United States now allows branches of foreign banks to participate in FedWire on terms closer to those afforded to domestic institutions, provided the home country of the foreign bank adheres to the Basle capital accord. Adherence to the accord would give host-country authorities greater confidence in the safety and soundness of the foreign bank. This approach, however, does not address the issue of systemic risk that arises when a foreign bank with a branch in the host country actually fails. Under our framework, capital requirements would already have been harmonized for purposes of safety and soundness for the entry and operation of branches. Extra measures would be needed to avoid systemic risk if this first line of defense proved inadequate.

CONSUMER PROTECTION. If a branch of a foreign bank accepts deposits of host-country residents, the host country has an interest in protecting the depositors against the possible failure of the foreign bank. To this end, a host country could require branches of foreign banks, or at least those that take "retail" deposits, to participate in its deposit insurance system. The problem with this approach, that is, using host-country rules, is that the exposure of the host-country insurer is dependent on home-country regulation and supervision of the bank. Harmonization of rules for safety and soundness could make this situation more acceptable; but because such rules cannot provide a 100 percent guarantee against failure, the host country might still be required to pay for the ineffectiveness of the home country's supervisory policies.

One solution to the problem of potential losses by the host-country insurer is to permit the host country to require branches of foreign banks to pledge readily marketable assets as a condition for insurance. In addition, the host country might require that branches of foreign banks maintain total assets that exceed total liabilities and that the assets not be excessively risky, a quasi "capital" requirement. In the event that a foreign bank failed, the pledged assets would be immediately available to host-country authorities to cover or reduce the losses of the insurer, or they would be available directly to uninsured local depositors. Although other branch assets would be subject to host-country liquidation, the "capital" requirement would help to ensure that such assets were sufficient to cover the claims of branch creditors, including those of the insurer. However, special host-country requirements for branch assets might unduly constrain the ability of the bank as a whole to operate in an efficient manner and, given harmonized capital requirements, would be unnecessary to maintain the safety and soundness of the bank.

Moreover, the effectiveness of these measures assumes that the host-country authorities have the legal power to seize branch assets and control their disposition, either through realizing on the pledge or putting the branch into liquidation. This assumption is not free from doubt. It depends on whether a branch is treated as a separate entity in a liquidation (host-country jurisdiction) or there is unity of the bankruptcy (home-country jurisdiction). If the home-country receiver asserts a claim to the assets of the entire bank, including the assets of foreign branches, the host country may not be able to dispose of the assets of the branch without causing conflict with the home country.

In practice, host countries may try to liquidate a branch of a failing foreign bank as if it were a separate entity. For example, in the United States, state or federal authorities have seized assets (in one case a building, in another large local interbank deposits) and used them to pay off local depositors and creditors; in one instance, a surplus was sent to the home-country authorities. Nonetheless, the home-country receiver may well consider all of the assets of the failed bank—including those booked at its foreign branches—to be within the jurisdiction of the home country. In the case of the 1974 near failure of Franklin National Bank, U.S. authorities persuaded the U.K. authorities to allow the U.S. receiver to take control of the London branch of the U.S. bank.

There is no generally accepted international rule in this area. The Basle Concordat deals with supervisory issues (it assigns primary responsibility for solvency to the home country and liquidity to the host country) and does not address assignment of responsibilities in the event of bankruptcy. Financial institutions are not covered by a bankruptcy convention recently agreed upon in the Council of Europe or by a draft EC convention still in longstanding negotiations.

If the home country has the legal power to control the disposition of all of the assets of a failed bank, including those at its foreign branches, the pledge and quasi capital requirements of the host country would be rendered ineffective. In this situation, a host-country insurer would be fully exposed to the risk of inadequate supervision by the home country. To reduce this exposure, the host country would need to have jurisdiction over the disposition of the branch assets. Thus, the use of host-country rules for deposit insurance requires use of host-country rules for bankruptcy (that is, the separate entity approach).

There are, however, significant drawbacks to this approach. Home-country depositors, or their insurers, may be deprived of claims to assets booked at foreign branches, and it is far from clear why host-country claims to such assets should be superior. Since the bank as a whole has gone bankrupt, fairness suggests that claims should be resolved in one collective proceeding in which similarly situated creditors are treated alike. In addition, dismemberment of the bank through host-country liquidations of branch assets may effectively prevent the home country from restructuring or selling the bank, thus interfering with the preservation of the bank's overall value. Nonetheless, the fact remains that it would be exceedingly difficult to achieve an international agreement providing for exclusive home-country jurisdiction over bank bankruptcies.

As an alternative to host-country deposit insurance, deposits in a branch of a foreign bank could be covered under the deposit protection scheme of its home country. For host countries, this raises the question of what amount of protection provided by the home-country scheme would be acceptable; for example, the level of coverage, the degree of risk-sharing by depositors, the types of deposits covered, and the speed and convenience of payouts. This question is further complicated by the fact that the lack of uniformity in deposit protection schemes is not the only factor contributing to differences among countries in protecting depositors. Other factors that can be equally important to host countries include government ownership of banks and central bank lending to or government recapitalization of private banks.

The concerns of the host country about the adequacy of depositor protection afforded by the home country could be resolved only by harmonization of deposit protection schemes. Indeed, the EC Commission is now considering whether to propose the home-country approach for Community branches of EC banks and, if so, what harmonization such an approach might entail. Beyond the Community, whether sufficient harmonization of deposit protection schemes exists or could ever be agreed upon is far more uncertain.

If harmonized and home-country rules were used for deposit insurance, home-country rules could then be used for bankruptcy. Because host-country authorities would not be providing insurance for deposits at branches of foreign banks, the host country would no longer need to have jurisdiction over the liquidation of the branch. Thus, home-country deposit insurance would work in tandem with home-country bankruptcy jurisdiction and avoid the drawbacks of the separate entity approach to bankruptcy. Whether, and if so to what extent, acceptance of the principle of the unity of the bankruptcy would require harmonization among nations on priorities of creditors is beyond the scope of this paper. Within the European Community, the Commission has proposed a "winding up" directive that would give home-country authorities exclusive responsibility for winding up branches of EC banks; this approach would work effectively with home-country deposit protection if that were to be proposed.

For deposit insurance, the Banking Matrix envisions a second-best solution: the application of host-country rules with special requirements for branches of foreign banks and agreement that, in the event of bankruptcy, the host country would have jurisdiction over the disposition of the assets of branches of foreign banks. Although this approach is theoretically inferior to the use of harmonized and home-country rules for deposit insurance and bankruptcy, we do not believe the alternative is realistically achievable in the foreseeable future. We would be happy to be proved wrong.

Subsidiaries

Unlike branches, subsidiaries are separately incorporated under the laws of host countries and are therefore similar to domestically owned banks. Subsidiaries of foreign banks have their own capital, which is within the regulatory and supervisory jurisdiction of host-country authorities. Because such subsidiaries are part of a multinational organization, however, a host country might still be concerned with the condition of a parent bank and the extent to which it might serve as a source of strength by standing ready to inject capital into its host-country subsidiary.

29

Entry. As with branches, the relevant policy goals for entry of subsidiaries are competition, and safety and soundness.

COMPETITIVE MARKETS. Promoting competitive markets requires that foreign ownership of domestic banks not be prohibited. But two major competitive issues do arise with respect to the establishment of subsidiaries. The first is whether nonbanking firms can establish banking subsidiaries in the host country. Some countries that limit the nonbanking powers of banks also limit the ownership of banks by nonbanking firms. The prohibition against nonbank ownership of banks has been justified on the grounds of either safety and soundness or competition. The arguments are that nonbanking parents cannot serve as a source of strength for their subsidiaries as well as banking parents can, and that the prohibition of ownership by nonbanks prevents concentrations of power and conflicts of interest. The issue of ownership of banks, like the question of nondiscriminatory restrictions on branch entry, might best be addressed through international harmonization of rules.

The second competitive issue regarding entry for subsidiaries is whether foreign banks can establish subsidiaries at multiple locations within the host country when domestic banks are not free to do so. Such geographic restrictions, even if applied to foreign banks on a nondiscriminatory basis, could be viewed as anticompetitive. This problem, like that which arises for branch entry, could be solved by international harmonization of intranational rules, for example, by prohibiting geographic restrictions.

When a country has a federal structure other difficulties appear. If it permits subnational governments, such as states or provinces, to define the scope of interstate banking, as the United States does for subsidiaries, certain problems may arise in dealing with foreign banks. Foreign banks may, for example, need to be "domesticated" by being assigned to a home state or region for the purpose of the application of host-country rules. A more serious problem arises if subnational governments discriminate between foreign and domestic banks, for example, by permitting only domestic banking organizations to acquire banks within their jurisdiction. Such policies violate the principle of nondiscriminatory treatment, and host countries with federal systems may have to resort to federal statutory or constitutional changes to resolve such problems.

Our approach to promoting competitive markets for the establishment of subsidiaries calls for host-country rules and harmonized rules, as indicated in the Banking Matrix. Harmonization may be necessary with respect to rules relating to ownership and geographic location. In other respects, application of nondiscriminatory host-country rules to the establishment of subsidiaries—in contrast to the establishment of branches—does not seem to compromise competition. Moreover, unlike the establishment of branches, the creation of host-country subsidiaries requires compliance with the corporate laws of the host country.

SAFETY AND SOUNDNESS. The goal of safety and soundness provides a justification for the host country to impose certain conditions on entry, such as capital requirements equivalent to those applied to domestic banks. If the source-of-strength doctrine is accepted, the host country's interest in the safety and soundness of the subsidiary's foreign parent is similar to its interest when the host-country entity is a branch. As a result, the host country may have an interest not only in the capitalization of the subsidiary but also in the capital adequacy of the parent banking institution. For example, the Federal Reserve Board requires foreign banks seeking to establish or acquire banking operations in the United States to meet "the same general standards of strength, experience and reputation" as are required of domestic banking organizations and to serve on a continuing basis as a source of strength to their banking operations in the United States.[11] Application of the source-of-strength doctrine would be facilitated by more widespread international harmonization of capital standards.

The Basle accord, in conformity with the earlier BIS agreement on consolidated supervision, envisions that for supervisory purposes home countries will apply bank capital requirements on a consolidated basis. Such consolidation would complement, but not replace, the capital requirements applied to a subsidiary by the host country. The purpose of applying home-country capital requirements on a consolidated basis is to ensure that the group as a whole has adequate capital to support all of its activities; and these requirements may affect the activities of subsidiaries. But a host country would nonetheless want to ensure that the subsidiary itself had adequate capital to support its activities. This is consistent with the host country's interest in the safety and soundness of its own banks.

The Banking Matrix, therefore, reflects our view that, to ensure safety and soundness, host-country rules should apply to the establishment of subsidiaries. But because we have recommended international harmonization of captial standards for branch entry, most countries would already be adhering to the same standards.

Operation. Both goals relevant to entry of subsidiaries—promoting competitive markets and ensuring safety and soundness—are, of course, also relevant to their operation. In general, the same considerations and rules apply.

COMPETITIVE MARKETS. One additional issue arises with respect to permissible activities of subsidiaries. Competition in a host country would be promoted by permitting subsidiaries to engage in at least the same activities as domestic banks; but it would be even further enhanced by permitting subsidiaries to conduct the same activities they are permitted at home. As in the case of branches, basic rules for permissible activities would need to be harmonized to avoid competitive inequalities. These considerations suggest that the entry in the matrix could be the same as that for branches, that is, home-country rules and harmonization.

But even the European Community is using *host*-country rules— that is, a policy of national treatment—for subsidiaries. However, the national treatment policy for subsidiaries is somewhat misleading. The Community relies on home-country rules—subject to the constraint of an agreed list of activities—to determine the permissible activities for branches and banks providing cross-border services. This serves as a tool for regulatory convergence. The almost inevitable harmonization of rules for permissible activities that will result from this process will also affect subsidiaries. Similarly, beyond the Community, if home-country and harmonized rules were used for branches, there would effectively be harmonized rules for subsidiaries.

The Banking Matrix reflects our choice of host-country and harmonized rules for operations of subsidiaries. We view harmonization as the critical element of this entry whether it occurs through de facto market pressures, through convergence resulting from negotiated harmonization only for branch activities, or through explicitly negotiated harmonization about the permissible activities of subsidiaries. We have entered host-country rather than home-country rules where harmonization has not occurred primarily on practical grounds because subsidiaries, unlike branches, are separately incorporated host-country entities.

OTHER POLICY GOALS. Because subsidiaries are separately incorporated in the host country, the remaining policy goals—avoiding systemic risk and consumer protection—can be furthered by treating the subsidiaries under host-country rules exactly like domestically owned banks. Measures to deal with systemic risk as well as consumer protection measures can be applied without regard to the ownership of a bank.

Overview of the Matrix

Our analysis, whose conclusions are set out in the Banking Matrix, relates the choice of rules governing international trade in banking services both to the means by which such services are provided and to the policy goals countries seek to achieve. The most obvious conclusion is that no single rule can be applied to all the combinations of methods and goals. Moreover, with the exception of disclosure requirements, no single rule can support a particular policy goal for every method by which the banking service is provided. The analysis also demonstrates that of all the goals, promoting competitive markets and ensuring the safety and soundness of banks depend most heavily on harmonization.

With some important exceptions, our analysis suggests that home-country rules should be applied to cross-border services, host-country rules to subsidiaries, and harmonized rules or special host-country rules to branches. For cross-border services, in general, host-country regulation—that is, national treatment—is not appropriate. Those services should be governed by home-country rules: They enhance competition, the systemic risk is small, and only the home country can provide deposit insurance. However, even for cross-border services, home-country rules do not adequately address safety and soundness and the disclosure aspect of consumer protection. If foreign banks solicited retail deposits from host-country residents, the host country would have a concern with safety and soundness that could be addressed through international harmonization of prudential standards. However, if the home country provided, through its own deposit insurance system, protection to such depositors that the host country considered adequate, the host country's concern with the prudential standards applied to the foreign bank would be lessened. This consideration serves to highlight a more general point about the analysis: The choice of rules for one combination of goals and methods may affect the choice for another.

In contrast to the rules for cross-border services, host-country rules are generally appropriate for subsidiaries. The reason is that subsidiaries can, for the most part, be regulated just as their domestic counterparts are without raising any special concerns about safety and soundness, systemic risk, or consumer protection. Application of the source-of-strength doctrine would be facilitated, however, by more widespread international harmonization of capital standards. In any event, as the matrix indicates, international harmonization of rules may be necessary to promote competitive markets with respect to both entry and operation of subsidiaries. Harmonization seems the most useful solution to the competitive problems raised by host-country restrictions on the ownership of subsidiaries conducting a banking business, on the geographic locations at which they can be initially established or subsequently operated, and on the services that they can provide. But harmonization would not be easy to accomplish: For example, it could require the United States to remove its restrictions on interstate banking, and it could require Japan and the United States to permit banks to offer securities services.

The treatment of foreign branches raises the most complicated questions. These arise because branches, though located and doing business in a host country, are an integral part of banks located in the home country. Thus, by their very nature, branches are subject to conflicting regulatory regimes that can be reconciled for the most part only through harmonized rules.

Our analysis suggests that ensuring safety and soundness and competitive markets when services are provided by branches of foreign banks requires harmonized rules, home-country rules where harmonization is not deemed necessary, and home-country enforcement. This is the EC approach under the Second Banking Directive. Competition, particularly with regard to geographic location and permissible activities, would be enhanced by this approach. The goal of safety and soundness requires harmonization of prudential regulations, but such regulations ultimately must be enforced by the home country. Harmonization of prudential rules is also important because it permits greater use of home-country rules to promote competitive markets. Once the goal of safety and soundness is assured, the main rationale for discriminatory restrictions on competition is removed. This is another example of the interdependence among the rules selected for the various combinations of methods and goals.

Our analysis further suggests that host countries might justifiably apply different rules to branches of foreign banks than to domestic banks for purposes of avoiding systemic risk and protecting depositors. Arguably, such policies might not be truly "discriminatory" because domestic banks and the branches of foreign banks might not be in "like situations," at least for these purposes. In any event, special treatment may be necessary to avoid the potential risk arising from participation by branches in host-country payment systems. Requiring branches to pledge or maintain marketable assets might also be justified to cover potential losses of host-country depositors or insurers. But such rules would be ineffective without host-country jurisdiction over the disposition of branch assets in the event of bank bankruptcies. Application of special host-country rules to protect host-country depositors could be avoided through harmonization of deposit insurance schemes and application of the home-country scheme to deposits in host-country branches; in that event, home-country rules should also be used for bankruptcy. Although this alternative is theoretically preferable, we did not adopt it in the matrix because of the considerable practical difficulties in achieving harmonization of deposit insurance schemes and in reaching an agreement providing for exclusive home-country jurisdiction over bank bankruptcies.

We can also analyze the way in which international banking services are provided from the perspective of each of the policy goals. For example, for systemic risk and deposit insurance, the matrix shows that quite different rules may be required for different forms of operation. Systemic risk is of minimal concern for cross-border services. For subsidiaries, systemic risk can be handled by the rules applicable to domestic banks because the subsidiaries are regulated for safety and soundness by the host country. In the case of branches, the host country must apply special rules.

With respect to deposit insurance, for cross-border services, home-country rules must govern because the foreign bank has no presence in the host country. Although the host country can require that domestic deposits at branches of foreign banks be insured, it then has an interest in ensuring that the branch has sufficient assets to cover potential payouts to depositors. As discussed above, these interests could be addressed by an agreement on host-country jurisdiction over branches in the event of bankruptcy. For separately incorporated subsidiaries, host-country rules for deposit insurance can readily be applied.

Harmonization of rules is important with regard to the policy goals of safety and soundness and competitive markets. Harmonized pruden-tial rules help protect depositors or insurers against bank failures. The Basle accord indicates that this approach is feasible, but harmonized capital requirements are only a first step. Other aspects of prudential supervision, such as examination and reporting requirements, are also important. Harmonized rules with respect to the powers of banks and the geographic locations at which they can operate would clearly pro-mote competitive markets. This is true both for subsidiaries and branches of foreign banks. In theory, one could allow subsidiaries to be governed by host-country rules; but as a practical matter, harmonizing rules that govern competition for branches will necessarily result in the same rules for subsidiaries if competitive equality between domestic banks and branches of foreign banks is to be maintained.

In stressing the need for harmonized rules for competition, we do not mean to prejudge the content of such rules. In other words, we are not using harmonization as a code word for deregulation. With regard to entry, however, harmonization for competitive purposes should involve removal of restrictive measures that limit market access. With regard to branch operations, efforts to harmonize competition rules might result in agreement to permit the same powers to banks as now specified by the EC's Second Banking Directive. If so, the result would be liberalization of existing rules in the United States and Japan. Although broadening powers would generally enhance competition if safety and soundness concerns were addressed, it might not always be possible politically. Nevertheless, without convergence of rules for powers of banks, problems in this area may continue to arise, with the risk of retaliatory actions that could curtail competition.[12] In the case of safety and soundness, harmonization could involve reregulation, such as strengthening capital requirements.

The Appropriate Forum

Our analysis suggests that an international framework for the provision of international banking services would require agreement both on basic principles—that is, whether host, home, or harmonized rules should apply in particular situations—and on the specifics of harmonized rules when that is the accepted principle. Achievement of such a framework, which goes considerably beyond the effort currently under way in the Uruguay Round, would, of course, require an international forum. In this section, we consider the ideal characteristics of such a forum and the extent to which existing international fora—the General Agreement on Tariffs and Trade, the Organisation for Economic Cooperation and Development, and the Bank for International Settlements—meet these criteria.

Characteristics of a Forum

An appropriate forum might (1) include only countries whose levels of development were sufficiently alike that they had similar interests in the liberalization of banking services; (2) include the relevant financial service regulators and finance ministry officials from such countries; and (3) have authority to formulate proposals, monitor their implementation, and resolve disputes. These characteristics flow directly from our previous analysis.

The appropriate group of countries. As our analysis shows, competition and safety and soundness considerations are important in establishing a conceptual framework for international banking. Thus, at the outset, the forum should perhaps consist primarily of developed countries that have a common interest in the extent to which their home-country banks can operate in each other's markets. It may be extremely difficult to get more than a few developing countries to accept the same competitive principles as developed countries, particularly with respect to the entry of foreign banks. Many of these countries are quite concerned with foreign domination, and they see little to gain from liberalization of the terms of entry of their banks into developed countries. Moreover, developed countries may be particularly concerned with safety and soundness problems that could arise from entry by banks from developing countries.

The forum should nevertheless have sufficient flexibility to accommodate a growing number of countries. For example, if a host country conditions entry for foreign banks on home-country acceptance and observance of certain internationally agreed supervisory standards, banks from countries not in the initial group but subsequently meeting such standards might be given the same rights of entry as those in the initial group.

Officials participating in the forum. The officials from the countries involved in devising an international framework would ideally include regulators of banking and other financial services (including central bankers) and finance ministry officials. Because of their expertise and previous experience in devising harmonization measures, such as those developed by the BIS Committee on Banking Regulations and Supervisory Practices, banking regulators are clearly essential to the development of the more extensive harmonization envisioned in our analysis.

Moreover, with regard to the goal of safety and soundness, banking regulators are the officials who would implement any agreed-upon rules.

An important part of an effort to develop the international framework we envision would involve a determination of the powers that foreign banks may exercise in host countries. As we have indicated, this determination turns upon questions of competition as well as those of safety and soundness. If banks are to be permitted to offer a broad range of financial services, the expertise of nonbanking regulators, such as securities and insurance regulators, will also be important in formulating international rules.

Moreover, in most countries, government officials other than regulators, such as those in finance ministries, deal with the formulation of policies regarding the basic structure of the financial system. To become effective, these policies often require legislative changes, and finance officials often take the lead in such a process. Although regulators clearly have an important role, their policy choices are frequently circumscribed by the broader legal framework for which the other government officials are responsible. Some of the harmonization issues that we have discussed, such as additional powers for banking organizations, would require legislative changes and would be highly political. These issues have the potential to affect the political and economic interests of the participating countries and thus require the involvement of finance ministry officials as well as financial service regulators.

Authority of the forum. Ideally, the forum would be more than a meeting place. It would be an international institution with delegated authority from participating countries that enabled it to reach decisions binding on participants and that permitted it to monitor implementation of its rules and resolve significant disputes about them. The supranational character of the European Community, as discussed above, has been important to the ability of the EC countries to harmonize certain features of their banking laws as part of the internal market program. Though the supranational structure of the Community goes far beyond what would be required for an international regulatory forum, any forum undertaking international harmonization would be strengthened to the extent it possessed some supranational authority.

As our analysis demonstrates, the forum would inevitably confront issues that go beyond banking, at least as narrowly conceived. It would have to deal with whether banks should have the power to offer securities and insurance services, and with the appropriate structure for regulating banks offering such services. These issues would necessarily overlap with other issues regarding such services—for example, disclosure requirements for cross-border securities offerings or capital requirements for nonbank securities firms. There would also be overlap with the macroeconomic measures required to realize the full benefits from developing an international framework for banking services—for example, liberalization of rules relating to capital movements.

The ideal international forum would have authority to deal with all issues involving financial services, but in practice it would be difficult to find one forum with such broad authority. Even on a national level, many countries have found it difficult to integrate different types of financial service regulation. A second-best, but more realistic alternative would be to have several fora whose efforts would be coordinated by a broader forum. For example, the BIS might deal with harmonization of capital requirements for securities activities of banks and coordinate with a broader forum that dealt with the powers of banks generally. Similarly, the International Monetary Fund or the OECD might serve as a specialized forum for rules governing capital movements. In principle, a specialized forum could also serve as the broader forum.

The Choice among Existing Fora

The creation of a new forum for developing an international framework for banking services along the lines we have suggested merits consideration. In the absence of a new institutional framework, the most likely fora for undertaking the effort are the GATT, the OECD, and the BIS. How well do these fora meet the ideal criteria?

The GATT. The GATT falls short of the ideal forum in several ways. One problem is that it comprises a large number of economically diverse countries, many of whom have little interest in liberalizing rules for financial services. In particular, few of the developing countries in the GATT are likely to agree to be bound by the same principles as developed countries. However, in accordance with an approach that has been suggested in the GATT negotiations on financial services, the developed countries and some of the more industrialized developing countries could try to reach agreement among themselves before trying to resolve their differences with other developing countries. Moreover, principles agreed to by a primary group of countries, in the GATT or elsewhere, might subsequently be applied to other countries whose banks are seeking to enter markets of countries in the original group. This broadening of application has already occurred in some instances with respect to the Basle accord.

Another problem with the GATT as a forum is that, for the most part, the participating officials are experts in trade in goods rather than in banking or other financial services. This emphasis was natural because, before the Uruguay Round, the GATT dealt solely with trade in goods. As this paper has suggested, liberalization of international trade in banking services raises complicated issues that are best handled by specialists. If the somewhat autonomous GATT Financial Services Body being discussed in the Uruguay Round negotiations were to be established, it could conceivably play a role in the development of an international framework for banking services of the sort suggested here.

The BIS. Though it is closer to the ideal forum for international trade in banking services than the GATT is, the BIS also has some drawbacks. The G-10 countries that are represented on the BIS Committee on Banking Regulations and Supervisory Practices have a common level of development; but the group may be too narrow because it excludes a number of developed countries with similar interests in international banking services. On the other hand, the BIS Committee includes banking regulators with substantial expertise and experience in harmonizing banking rules on an informal and nonbinding basis; they have negotiated the risk-based capital accord, the Concordats, and the minimum standards for interbank netting schemes. However, the BIS does not formally include other financial service regulators or finance ministry officials, whose participation would be necessary to reach government-to-government agreements as opposed to understandings among bank regulators.

The BIS could play an extremely useful role in the international regulatory framework we have described as a specialized forum for issues involving safety and soundness and systemic risk. Other countries could be brought into the discussions of these issues after the BIS had formulated preliminary proposals. The proposals of the expanded group of banking officials could then feed into a broader forum that included government officials more attuned to competition and consumer protection considerations. Similar input to the broader forum could also be made by other financial service regulators.

The OECD. The OECD has some advantages as a forum for the purposes discussed in this paper. Currently, it comprises twenty-four countries at relatively similar levels of development.[13] Also, most of the relevant government officials from the finance ministries, central banks, and supervisory authorities regularly attend meetings of its committees or the working groups established under its committees.

The OECD also has some experience with nonbinding harmonization of national laws. In the 1970s, the Committee on Financial Markets issued recommendations that came close to harmonization of rules in the area of operation of unit trusts (mutual funds) and disclosures applicable to publicly offered securities. In addition, the Committee on Fiscal Affairs has developed a model tax convention to avoid double taxation. For the most part, however, the OECD has sought to establish the principle of nondiscriminatory application of host-country rules rather than dismantle nondiscriminatory barriers that could involve changes in the regulatory framework of a host country. Some of the latter work could be carried on by specialized fora such as the BIS. The OECD could thus be the broad forum that coordinated the efforts of other groups.

One problem with the OECD is that its members, unlike those in the European Community, have not surrendered any sovereignty to it. Decision making, as in the GATT, must be unanimous. Moreover, although its rules are legally binding, the OECD lacks a strong mechanism for settling disputes. If it were to play the role of the broad forum, its ability to resolve disputes would have to be greatly strengthened, a move that would involve a major change of style for the organization. The OECD would also need to find ways of including nonmember countries that meet certain criteria based, for example, on regulatory and supervisory standards as well as liberalization of access.

Conclusion

This paper sets forth a conceptual framework for analyzing international trade in banking services and uses it to suggest rules applicable to various forms of such trade. Determining the appropriate rules requires systematic examination of the policy goals involved in the regulation of banks, as well as of the methods by which international banking services are provided. Our framework—with the principles of host-country, home-country, or harmonized rules—enables one to go beyond conventional verbal formulations, such as national treatment or effective market access, that often avoid or paper over underlying concerns and the complexities of the issues. Although reasonable people may differ over the details of our analysis and the solutions we propose for each combination of policy goals and methods of providing services, the systematic approach embodied in the matrix that relates the choice of rules to both the goals and the methods remains useful. Indeed, a similar approach could be used for other financial services, such as securities and insurance.

From the perspective of this paper, the establishment of an appropriate international regulatory framework for trade in banking services is an ongoing, long-term effort. The current efforts of the Uruguay Round could be viewed as an important beginning. Our analysis suggests that consideration should be given to continuing this work in the OECD or the GATT, either of which could serve as the forum for agreement on the appropriate principles and could participate in or coordinate the efforts of other specialized fora in arriving at harmonized rules where they are deemed necessary.

Endnotes

1 See Sydney J. Key, "Is National Treatment Still Viable? U.S. Policy in Theory and Practice." *Journal of International Banking Law*, vol. 5, no. 9 (Winter 1990), pp. 365–381. An earlier version of this paper was presented at a *Conference on World Banking and Securities Markets after 1992*, International Center for Monetary and Banking Studies, Geneva, February 1990.

2 See Sydney J. Key, "Mutual Recognition: Integration of the Financial Sector in the European Community," *Federal Reserve Bulletin*, vol. 75 (September 1989), pp. 591–609.

3 Robin Leigh-Pemberton, "Ownership and control of UK banks," *Bank of England Quarterly Bulletin*, vol. 27 (November 1987), p. 526.

4 The Group of Ten, or G-10, actually consists of twelve countries: Belgium, Canada, France, Germany, Italy, Japan, Luxembourg, the Netherlands, Sweden, Switzerland, the United Kingdom, and the United States.

5 The original 1975 Concordat is reproduced in International Monetary Fund, *International Capital Markets: Recent Developments and Short-Term Prospects, 1981*, Occasional Paper No. 7 (August 1981), pp. 29–32. The 1983 revised Concordat is reproduced in 22 *I.L.M.* 901 (1983).

6 See Hal S. Scott, "A Payment System Role for a European System of Central Banks," in Committee for the Monetary Union of Europe, *For a Common Currency*, pp. 77–106 (The Committee, 1990). A modified version of this paper was published in *Payment Systems Worldwide*, vol. 1, no. 3 (Autumn 1990), pp. 3–15.

7 The standards were part of the "Lamfalussy Report;" see Bank for International Settlements, *Report of the Committee on Interbank Netting Schemes of the Central Banks of the Group of Ten Countries* (BIS, November 1990).

8 Another example of loss-limitation measures is the limitation on the amount a consumer may have to pay in charges on a lost bank card.

9 The Group of Seven, or G-7, consists of Canada, France, Germany, Italy, Japan, the United Kingdom, and the United States.

10 Second Council Directive of 15 December 1989 on the coordination of laws, regulations and administrative provisions relating to the taking up and pursuit of the business of credit institutions and amending Directive 77/780/EEC (89/646/EEC), 32 *O.J. Eur. Comm.* (No. L 386) 1 (1989).

11 See Board of Governors of the Federal Reserve System, "Supervision and Regulation of Foreign-based Bank Holding Companies," Policy Statement, February 23, 1979, F.R.R.S. 4-835. See also Regulation Y, 12 C.F.R. §225.4(a)(1) and Board of Governors of the Federal Reserve System, "Unsound Banking Practices—Failure to Act as Source of Strength to Subsidiary Banks," Policy Statement, April 24, 1987, F.R.R.S. 4–878.

12 See Hal S. Scott, "La notion de réciprocité dans la proposition de deuxième directive de coordination bancaire," *Révue du Marché Commun*, no. 323 (January 1989), pp. 45–56.

13 Australia, Austria, Belgium, Canada, Denmark, Finland, France, Germany, Greece, Iceland, Ireland, Italy, Japan, Luxembourg, the Netherlands, New Zealand, Norway, Portugal, Spain, Sweden, Switzerland, Turkey, the United Kingdom, and the United States.

Group of Thirty
Members

Rt. Hon. Lord Richardson of Duntisbourne KG
Chairman, Group of Thirty; Chairman, Morgan Stanley International

Mr. Geoffrey Bell
Executive Secretary, Group of Thirty; Chairman, Guinness Mahon Holdings; President, Geoffrey Bell & Company

Sir Roderick Carnegie
Hudson Conway Limited, Australia

Mr. Richard Debs
Chairman, R. A. Debs & Company

Sr. Guillermo de la Dehesa
Consejero Delegado, Banco Pastor

Professor Gerhard Fels
Director, Institut der Deutschen Wirtschaft

Dr. Jacob A. Frenkel
Economic Counsellor and Director of Research Department, The International Monetary Fund

Dr. Wilfried Guth
Member of the Supervisory Board, Deutsche Bank

Mr. Erik Hoffmeyer
Chairman of the Board of Governors, Danmarks Nationalbank

Mr. Thomas S. Johnson
President, Manufacturers Hanover

Professor Peter B. Kenen
Director, International Finance Section, Department of Economics, Princeton University

Professor Paul Krugman
Professor of Economics, Massachusetts Institute of Technology

Mr. Yoh Kurosawa
President, The Industrial Bank of Japan

Mr. Anthony Loehnis
Vice Chairman, S. G. Warburg & Co., Ltd.

Mr. Stephen Marris
Senior Associate Scholar, Institute for International Economics

Mr. Michiya Matsukawa
Senior Advisor to the President, Nikko Securities Co., Ltd.

Mr. Shijuro Ogata
Deputy Governor, The Japan Development Bank

Dr. Sylvia Ostry
Chairman, Centre for International Studies, The University of Toronto

Dr. Tommaso Padoa-Schioppa
Deputy Director General, Banca d'Italia

Mr. Robert V. Roosa
Partner, Brown Brothers Harriman & Co.

Mr. Anthony M. Solomon
Director, S. G. Warburg Group

Mr. Tasuku Takagaki
President, The Bank of Tokyo, Ltd.

Mr. Charles R. Taylor
Executive Director, Group of Thirty

Mr. Jean-Claude Trichet
le Directeur du Trésor, France

Mr. Paul Volcker
Chairman, James Wolfensohn, Inc.

Mr. Rodney B. Wagner
Vice-Chairman, Credit Policy Committee, J. P. Morgan & Co.

Dr. Marina v N. Whitman
Vice-President & Group Executive, General Motors Corporation

———————

Dr. H. Johannes Witteveen
Honorary Chairman of the Group of Thirty; Advisor to the Board of Managing Directors, Amsterdam-Rotterdam Bank NV

Mr. John Heimann
Treasurer, Group of Thirty; Vice Chairman, Merrill Lynch Capital Markets

Group of Thirty
Publications

Reports:

Toward a Less Unstable International Monetary System
The Reserve Assets Study Group. 1980

Foreign Exchange Markets Under Floating Rates
The Exchange Markets Participants' Study Group. 1980

Balance-of-Payments Problems of Developing Countries
The Capital Movements and the Growth of International Indebtedness Study Group. 1981

The Outlook for International Bank Lending
The Capital Movements and the Growth of International Indebtedness Study Group. 1981

Reserve Currencies in Transition
Robert V. Roosa, et al. 1982

How Central Banks Manage Their Reserves
The Multiple Reserve Currency Study Group. 1982

How Bankers See the World Financial Market
The International Banking Study Group. 1982

Risks in International Bank Lending
The International Banking Study Group. 1982

Bank Supervision Around the World
Richard Dale. 1982

The Future of the International Oil Market
Edwin A. Deagle, Jr. 1983

The IMF and Private Markets
Committee on International Banking. 1983

Commercial Banks and the Restructuring of Cross-Border Debt
M. S. Mendelsohn. 1983

The Mexican Rescue
Joseph Kraft. 1984

Economic Co-operation from the Inside
Marjorie Deane and Robert Pringle. 1984

Foreign Direct Investment 1973–87
The Office of the Group of Thirty. 1984

The Foreign Exchange Market in the 1980s
The Foreign Exchange Market Study Group. 1985

Countertrade in the World Economy
Robert V. Roosa, et al. 1985

Outlook for Mineral Commodities
R. H. Carnegie. 1986

Inflation Stabilization with Incomes Policy Support
Rudiger Dornbusch and Mario Henrique Simonsen, with discussion by Mario Brodersohn, Michael Bruno, G. G. Johnson. 1987

Finance for Developing Countries
Richard A. Debs, David L. Roberts, Eli M. Remolona. 1987

International Macroeconomic Policy Co-ordination
Policy Co-ordination Study Group. 1988

Perestroika: A Sustainable Process for Change
John P. Hardt and Sheila N. Heslin, with commentary by Oleg Bogomolov. 1989

The Risks Facing the World Economy
The Risks Facing the World Economy Study Group. 1991

Financing Eastern Europe
Richard A. Debs, Harvey Shapiro and Charles Taylor, 1991

Special Reports:

Clearance and Settlement Systems in the World's Securities Markets
Steering & Working Committees of the Securities Clearance and Settlement Study. 1988

Clearance and Settlement Systems: Status Reports, Spring 1990
Various Authors. 1990

Clearance and Settlement Systems: Status Reports, Year-End 1990
Various Authors. 1991

Occasional Papers:

1. **Exchange Rates, Domestic Prices and the Adjustment Process**
   Peter B. Kenen and Clare Pack. 1980

2. **Credit Creation in the Euromarket:**
   Alternative Theories and Implications for Control
   Alexander K. Swoboda. 1980

3. **Views of Inflation in the United States**
   Herbert Stein. 1980

4. **Energy in the 1980s—An Analysis of Recent Studies**
   Edwin A. Deagle, Jr., Bijan Mossavar-Rahmani, Richard Huff. 1981

5. **"Overshooting" in the Foreign Exchange Market**
   Richard M. Levich. 1981

6. **The Role of Official Intervention**
   Michael Mussa. 1981

7. **Co-ordination of National Economic Policies**
   Jacques Polak. 1981

8. **Gradualism vs. Shock Therapy**
   William Fellner, et al. 1981

9. **Policy Choice and Economic Structure**
   John B. Taylor. 1982

53